Are You Smarter Than Eight 7th Graders?

Let's See!

Mrs. Morrell's 7th Grade English Class at Spring Creek Academy:

Maya

Nikki

Gabe

Brad

Henry

Joshua

Gustavo

Nick

For information, address requests to:

Mrs. Karen Morrell, Spring Creek Academy

6000 Custer Rd, Plano, TX, 75023.

ISBN 978-0-578-07785-7

First Edition: March 2011

Table of Contents

Interesting Facts about Eight Fascinating States - ALASKA

I hope you enjoy these facts I have gathered.

•

- Alaska was purchased from Russia for 2 cents an acre.
- The state motto of Alaska is "North to the Future!"
- The state flower of Alaska is the "Forget-me-not."
- The state fish of Alaska is the "King Trout."
- The state sport of Alaska is known as "Dog Mushing."
- In Alaska, the rest of the United States of America is referred to as "Lower 48."
- Alaska is home to more than three million ducks.

- The state insect of Alaska is actually the Dragonfly.
- Alaska is known to be larger than the next four largest states combined.
- Alaska is only 50 miles from Russia.
- In 1958, in Lituya Bay, Alaska, a wave caused by earthquakes generated a tsunami over 1,700 ft. high, which is bigger than a skyscraper.
- The largest cabbage in Alaska was 90 pounds.
- In 1951, Alaska was not considered a state of the United States of America.
- The wooly mammoth is the state fossil of Alaska.
- In Alaska, the moose is the state animal.
- The tallest mountain is Mt. McKinley.
- In Nome one may not roam the city with a bow and arrow.
- It is considered an offense to feed alcoholic beverages to a moose.
- Alaska doesn't allow sugar gliders as pets.
- Alaska origin name is Aleut meaning "Mainland."

- In Alaska a drunken person cannot enter a bar.
- Clowns are not allowed anywhere in Alaska.
- It is illegal to eat live eels anywhere in public.
- You can shoot a bear in Alaska, but not wake one up to take a picture of him.
- *Ulu*, a fan-shaped knife used for chopping meat.
- *Quiviut*, wool from an Alaska musk ox.
- The state tree in Alaska is known as the Sitka Spruce.
- A person cannot live in a trailer as it is being hauled across the city.
- Intentionally avoiding walking on the cracks in the pavement is illegal.
- Bartenders cannot serve drinks if they are drunk themselves.
- A person may only carry a concealed slingshot if that person has received the appropriate license.
- Owners of flamingos may not let their pet into barber shops, or any other animal.
- Persons may not allow "attractive nuisances" to exist in Alaska, Soldotna.

- In Alaska no one may tie their dog to the roof of a car.
- Employees of bars cannot let their bartender serve while they are drunk themselves.
- It is against the law to attempt to break any law in title 9 of the code.

Alaskan Dog Mushing Facts

- The Iditarod Sled Dog Race, held every first Saturday in March in Alaska since 1973, has popularized the sport.
- Mushers come to Alaska from other parts of the United States.
- Every winter Europeans come to Fairbanks to train on the hundreds of miles of well-groomed trails.
- The race has a ceremonial start in Anchorage, then restart occurs somewhere else.
- The 1,000 mile Yukon Quest International Sled Dog Race is the biggest long-distance race of the year in Fairbanks.

- Run in February, its trail ran in the Canada-to-Alaska direction in 1998 to commemorate the 1898 Gold Rush, although it usually switches directions between Fairbanks and Whitehorse, Canada every year.
- There are two more major Dog Mushing events in Fairbanks, both held in March.
- The first is the Limited North America Championship, a three-day series of sprint sled dog and skijoring races.
- The second is the oldest continuously run sled dog race. It is the Open North American Championship, a three-day series of races beginning and ending in Downtown Fairbanks, which draw the world's fastest mushers.
- Many residents keep two or more dogs for recreational Dog Mushing.
- Mushing is a year around activity. When there is no snow, mushers exercise and train their dogs using sleds with wheels.

Alaskan Moose Facts

- The Alaskan Bull Moose can become to 1,000 to 1,600 pounds when they are adult males, females on the other hand can be from 800 to 1,300 pounds when adults.

- Cow moose generally breed at 28 months, though some may breed as young as 16 months. Cows give birth to twins 15 to 75 percent of the time, and triplets may occur once in every 1,000 births. The incidence of twinning is directly related to range conditions. A cow moose *will* defend her newborn calf vigorously.

- Calves begin taking solid food a few days after birth. They are weaned in the fall at the time the mother is breeding again. The maternal bond is generally maintained until calves are 12 months old at which time the mother aggressively chases her offspring from the immediate area just before she gives birth.

- During fall and winter, moose consume large quantities of willow, birch, and aspen twigs. In some areas, moose actually establish a “hedge” or browse line 6 to 8 feet above the ground by clipping most of the terminal shoots of favored food species. Spring is the time of grazing as well as browsing. Moose eat a variety of foods, particularly sedges, equisetum, pond weeds, and grass.

ARIZONA

Arizona is a great state and it's one of my favorites. Before I knew all of the cool things about Arizona, I thought it was a boring state, but the more I read about it, the more appealing it became. I hope you think it is too.

When people discovered Arizona, they had no idea how many Native Americans that there were in Arizona.

There are about 21 different federally recognized tribes in Arizona.

The more famous ones include the Apache, Caddo, Cahuilla, Cherokee, Comanche, Kiowa, and the Navajo.

These tribes were also the reason behind some of the hundreds of ghost stories in Arizona.

One of the famous ghost stories is about a ghost town, which was a silver deposit that was found in the desert, but then the Indians invaded and most of the people died. Today, some people still believe that the spirits of the people haunt the place.

Many famous people were born in Arizona. Some of them are:

Barry Morris Goldwater. He was a Senator for the United States. He was born in Phoenix, Arizona.

Joseph Adam Jonas (Joe Jonas). He is in a pop band with both of his brothers. He was born in Casa Grande, Arizona.

Jordan Sparks. She was on American Idol and is now a famous singer. She was born in Phoenix, Arizona.

Earl John Hindman. He was an actor who is best known for his role in the T.V. show, "Home Improvement". He was born in Bisbee, Arizona.

Rex Elvie Allen. He was an American song writer an actor who was best known for being the voice narrating the story in many Disney cartoons. He was born in Willcox, Arizona.

Steven Spielberg. He is a famous American movie director. He wasn't born in Arizona but he was raised in Phoenix almost all of his life.

Joan Ganz Cooney who is the producer of Sesame Street, and was born in Phoenix, Arizona.

- The Arizona state motto is "Ditat Deus", which means "God Enriches".
- The name Arizona came from the Native American word *Arizonac,* meaning "Little Spring"
- Arizona leads the nation in copper production.
- Petrified wood is the state fossil.
- Arizona is home to the Grand Canyon.
- The ringtail is the state mammal.
- Turquoise is the official state gemstone.
- There are about 5 different big canyons in Arizona besides the Grand Canyon.
- Four Corners is located in Arizona, New Mexico, Colorado, and Utah, is noted as the place when you can stand in four states at the same time.
- The world's largest solar telescope is located in Arizona.
- At one time camels were used to transport material across Arizona.
- A person from Arizona is known as an Arizonian.

- The state song is “Arizona!”
- The state colors of Arizona are blue and old gold.
- A meteor crashed into the Earth’s surface at 5 to 10 miles per second about 50,000 years ago in the middle of Arizona.
- You can’t walk through a hotel lobby in spurs in Arizona.
- You could get up to 25 years in prison for cutting down a cactus in Arizona.
- Once in Arizona, some people at the University of Arizona wanted to see what the effects of drugs were and what would happen when they gave it to spiders. So then one day, they gave some spiders different drugs including; alcohol, cannabis, cocaine, crystal methane, marijuana, and other drugs. They saw the different effects of the drugs so they could identify them. Each of the spiders died from some sort of spider overdose.

  When I read about this, I was wondering how they got drugs because they are only in college.

- If you commit a misdemeanor in Wilcox, Arizona while wearing a red mask it is considered a felony.

Many movies were shot in Arizona. Arizona is manly an ideal place for westerns but many other movies were shot there, the more famous movies of all of these are:

- Forrest Gump
- Many of the Star Trek films
- Transformers
- Many of Clint Eastwood's films
- Casablanca
- Three Kings
- Contact
- Easy Rider
- Bill & Ted's Excellent Adventure & their Bogus Journey
- Wayne's World
- Psycho
- Taxi
- The Karate Kid

- Star Wars IV & VI
- Spaceballs
- And at last, The Shawshank Redemption

Arizona is home to the "aircraft bone yards". This is a place where airplanes go and die. That is what many people believe around that area. People go to the middle of nowhere in Arizona just to see a lot of airplane debris. Some people think that is where military projects went on and others think it is where airplanes go to die. Some people even reported planes crashing into the pile of airplanes.

Five ways unicorns and Phoenix, Arizona are alike:

- The unicorn and the phoenix are mythical creatures and the phoenix is how the city of Phoenix got its name.
- Sightings of unicorns go back to 200 B.C. when the Native Americans living around Phoenix said they saw unicorns.

- Unicorns like mud, and every year in one suburb of Phoenix, they have a mud festival.
- Unicorns live in forests and north of Phoenix there is a big forest.
- Last, Noah forgot to load two unicorns onto his ship a legend says that the unicorns flew west to find land and after the storm stopped they landed in the mud of Arizona.

CALIFORNIA

The Sunshine state has more than meets the eye. Full of fun facts and funky laws, California is an odd and exciting place.

- Ice cream may not be eaten while standing on the sidewalk in Carmel.
- More avocados are grown in Fallbrook than any other place in the U.S.
- It is prohibited to sleep in a parked vehicle in Cathedral City.
- California grows 99.5 percent of all the dates grown in the U.S.
- If you're a woman in Carmel, by law you can't wear high-heels.
- California produces over 17 million gallons of wine a year.
- Mt. Whitney in California is the highest peak in the continental U.S.

- Since 1937, when it opened, more then 1,200 people have fallen to their deaths off the Golden Gate Bridge in San Francisco.
- If you are classified as "Ugly", you can't walk down any street in San Francisco.
- If you want to keep a rhinoceros as a pet, you must get a $100 license first.
- The tallest tree in the world, at 369 feet, is in the Humboldt Redwook State Park.
- Death Valley, at 282 feet below sea level, is the lowest point in the U.S.
- The hottest day ever in the U.S. was on July 10, 1913, at Death Valley. The temperature reached 135 degrees.
- If you live in San Diego and don't take down your Christmas lights by February second, you could be fined up to $250.
- It is against the law to ride a bicycle in a swimming pool in Baldwin Park.
- In Lodi, it is illegal to shoot 'Silly String" at parade participants.

- It is illegal to herd more than 2,000 sheep down Hollywood Boulevard at one time.
- In Blythe, you are not allowed to wear cowboy boots unless you own at least two cows.
- In Long Beach, putting anything other than your car in your garage is illegal.
- It is against the law to curse on a mini golf course in Long Beach.
- In Redlands, motor vehicles may not drive on city streets unless a man with a lantern is walking in front of it.
- It is against the law for roosters to crow in the city limits in Ontario.
- It is illegal to walk a camel down Palm Canyon Drive between the hours of 4 and 6 p.m. in Palm Springs.
- California has the most national parks in the U.S.
- It is illegal to clean your car with used underwear in San Francisco.
- In California, it's illegal to try and stop a child from playfully jumping over puddles of water.

- California is the number one dairy state having passed Wisconsin in 1993.
- California grows enough strawberries to circle the world 15 times in one year.
- Dorris, California, is home to the tallest flagpole in the world.
- One of every eight music festivals is held in California.

MINNESOTA

Minnesota Fun Facts

Did you know the state of 10,000 lakes, has more than 10,000 lakes? According to the Minnesota Department of Natural Resources, it actually has 11,842.

- Minnesota has 9 lakes named *Bass*, 7 named *Big*, (27 with the word "Big" in them), 12 named *Clear*, 11 named *Eagle*, 7 named *Elbow*, 7 named *Fish*, 3 of which are all in Otter Tail, 33 with the word "little", 26 named *Long*, (5 in Otter Tail as well), one in Otter Tail named *McDonald*, 3 named *Mud*, 1 named *Ox Yoke*, 1 named *Potato*, 10 named *Rice*, 11 named *Round*. In Pope, MN, there's a lake named *Scandinavian* and 2 named *Lake Spoon*.

Spoon, Really? SPOON!?

- The state capital is St. Paul, and not Minneapolis.
- Minnesota, as of 2010, has around 5.2 million residents.
- Minnesota has 87 counties.
- Largest city in Minnesota is Minneapolis.
- The state bug is the Monarch Butterfly.
- The state bird is the Common Loon.
- The state fish is the Walleye.
- The state muffin is the blueberry.
- The state drink is milk.
- Minneapolis's Mall Of America, has 9.5 million square feet.
- Minnesota has more coastline than California, Florida and Hawaii combined!
- Minneapolis has the highest number of golfers per capita than any other city in the US.
- The first bone marrow transplant, and the first open heart surgery were done in Minnesota.

- Minnesota is the state in which the I-35 bridge collapse happened in 2007.
- Minnesota's population consists of less than .1% Hawaiian.

Famous People From Minnesota

Roger Nelson (Prince)

Richard Sears

Charles Schulz

Charles Lindbergh

Marion Barber

Harry Blackmun

Warren Burger

Pete Doctor

William O. Douglas

Pierce Butler

Coen Brothers

Seymour Cray

Bob Dylan

Mike Farrell

F. Scott Fitzgerald

Al Franklin

Judy Garland

Paul Getty

Terry Gilliam

Billy Graham

Peter Graves

Garrison Keillor

Jessica Lange

John Madden

Eugene McCarthy

John Pillsbury

Winona Ryder

Laura Ingalls Wilder

Famous Minnesota Companies

3M

Best Buy

Caribou Coffee

Cirrus Aviation

Cub Foods

Geek Squad

General Mills Inc.

Hormel Foods

Land O Lakes

Greyhound Lines

Northwest Airlines

Pillsbury

Pepsi America

Travelers Insurance

NEW YORK

New York is an exquisite place to be. Whether you're in the bustling city or in the peaceful suburbs you're sure to learn something interesting and new. That's why I chose to do this state. Hope you like it!

- The New York state flower is the rose.
- New York's bird is the bluebird.
- The state tree is a sugar maple.
- The capital of New York is Albany.
- New York's motto is Excelsior or "Ever Upward".
- Its nickname is "The Empire State".
- Its state animal is the beaver.
- The state song is "I Love New York".
- The state fruit is apple which is why the call the city "The Big Apple".

- Citizens in New York can not greet each other by putting their thumb on their nose and wiggling their fingers.
- You can be fined $25 dollars for flirting.
- If you jump off a building you get the death penalty.
- Slippers are not permitted to be worn after 10 p.m.
- It's against the law for people to slurp their soup.
- There are about 8.4 million people in New York City.
- There are about 19.5 million people in the state of New York.
- In 2010 they have about 3,715 hybrid taxis in the city.
- New York City is the second place movies are filmed the most.
- The city's 39 biggest theatres are known as "Broadway".
- Broadway has over 500 seats in each theatre.

- The busiest place in New York is Times Square. Even at 1 in the morning the streets are packed with thousands of people bumping into each other.
- 40 million people visit New York City every year.

OKLAHOMA

Overwhelming Oklahoma - Oklahoma is an exciting state with a lot of history. Here are some cool facts about Oklahoma.

- Oklahoma entered the Union on November 16, 1907.
- Oklahoma's capital is Oklahoma City.
- Oklahoma means "Red People".
- Oklahoma's nickname is "The Sooner State".
- Oklahoma's state tree is the Redbud.
- Oklahoma's state bird is the Scissor-Tailed Flycatcher.
- Oklahoma's state flower is the Mistletoe.
- Oklahoma's state game bird is Wild Turkey.
- Oklahoma's state animal is the Bison.
- Oklahoma's state furbearer is the Raccoon.

- Oklahoma's state reptile is the Collared Lizard.
- Oklahoma's state song is "Oklahoma!"
- Oklahoma has 51 state parks.
- Oklahoma's state motto is "Labor omnia vincit" (Labor conquers all things).
- Oklahoma is famous for the National Cowboy Hall of Fame and the Will Rogers Memorial.

Top Casinos - Because Oklahoma was settled by Native American tribes, they have a lot of casinos. Here are the most well-known in the state:

- Winstar Casino
- Riverwind Casino
- Comanche Red River Casino
- Lucky Star Casino
- Choctaw Casino

Oklahoma has some of the most prestigious colleges in the country. Here are a few:

- University of Oklahoma
- Oklahoma State University
- University of Central Oklahoma
- Oral Roberts University
- Oklahoma City University
- University of Tulsa
- Southwestern Oklahoma State University
- Oklahoma Baptist University
- Cameron University
- Langston University
- Northeastern State University
- Oklahoma Wesleyan University
- East Central University
- Rogers State University
- Saint Gregory's University

Quite a few famous people have come from Oklahoma. Many of them are country singers and athletes.

- Mickey Mantle (Baseball).
- Garth Brooks (Singer).
- James Garner (Actor).
- Oral Roberts (Evangelist).
- Will Roberts (Humorist).
- Jim Thorpe (Athlete).
- Toby Keith (Singer).
- Johnny Bench (Baseball).
- Reba McEntire (Singer).
- Paul Harvey (Broadcaster).

Oklahoma has great weather for golf, and also great courses.

Top Public Golf Courses in Oklahoma:

- Forest Ridge Golf Club
- Jimmie Austin/OU Golf Course
- Chickisaw Point
- Lincoln Park West
- Cedar Creek

- Battle Creek
- Coffee Creek
- Bailey Ranch
- Stone Creek

Top Private Golf Courses in Oklahoma:

- Oak Tree Golf Club
- Golf Club of Oklahoma
- Cedar Ridge
- Hillcrest
- Oklahoma City Golf & Country Club
- Tulsa CC
- Oak Tree East
- Dornick Hills
- Twin Hills

TEXAS

Texas is a marvelous state. Here are some interesting facts about it:

- State Bird: Mockingbird
- State Tree: Pecan
- State Flower: Bluebonnet
- Texas was the 28th state of the U.S. and was admitted on December 29th, 1845
- State Capital: Austin
- State Nickname: Lone Star State
- State Motto: Friendship
- State Song: "Texas, Our Texas"
- State Mammal(large): Texas Longhorn
- State Mammal(small): Armadillo
- State Flying Mammal: Mexican Free-tailed Bat
- State Insect: Monarch Butterfly
- State Reptile: Texas Horned Lizard

- State Fish: Guadalupe Bass
- State Shell: Lightning Whelk
- State Plant: Prickly Pear Cactus
- State Grass: Sideoats Grama
- State Shrub: Chinese Crepe Myrtle
- State Fruit: Red Grapefruit
- State Vegetable: Sweet Onion
- State Fiber: Cotton
- State Dinosaur: Pleurocoelus
- State Stone: Petrified Palmwood
- State Gem: Texas Blue Topaz
- State Dish: Chili
- State Pepper: Jalapeno
- State Ship: Battleship Texas

WASHINGTON

Here are all the facts you need to know about Washington! From general information, to the famous people who were born there! Hope you enjoy!

- Washington has 39 counties
- Population- 6,664,195
- Capital- Olympia
- Nickname- Evergreen State
- Mottos- Eventually; By and By
- State Bird- Gold Finch
- State Insect- Green Darner Dragonfly
- State Fruit- Apple
- State Tree-Western Hemlock
- Washington produces more apples than any other state.

- Spokane, Washington was the smallest city to ever host a World's Fair in 1974.
- Washington was the 42nd state to be admitted to the Union on November 11th,1889.
- Washington was named after the 1st president of the United States, George Washington.
- Washington is also a state with many firsts. The world's first gas station opened in Washington in 1907, and Seattle was the first city to play a Beatles song on the radio in the United States.
- Washington is also home to many famous industries, including Starbucks, Microsoft, and Boeing, who made the Lunar Rover.

One of the most famous events that ever happened in Washington was the eruption of Mt. Saint Helens. On May 18, 1980, the northeast face of Mt. St. Helens exploded outward. The eruption flattened the forests for many miles, killed 57 people, flooded the Columbian River with ash and mud, and blanketed large parts of Washington in ash.

Let's take a look at the famous people who were born in Washington.

- Jimi Hendrix, rock musician- Seattle
- Bing Crosby, musician- Tacoma
- Bob Barker, TV host- Darrington
- Bill Gates, creator of Microsoft- Seattle
- Adam West, actor/comedian- Walla Walla
- Kenny Loggins, singer/songwriter- Aberdeen
- Carol Channing, actress- Seattle
- Hillary Swank, actress- Bellingham
- William Boeing, aircraft manufacturer- Seattle
- Kurt Cobain, lead singer of Nirvana- Aberdeen
- Glenn Beck, radio/television host- Seattle
- Fred Couples, pro golfer- Seattle
- John Elway, football player- Port Angeles
- Chris Cornell, singer- Seattle

Weird, Weirder, and Weirdest

Weird Town Names

"What town do you live in?" "Slickpoo, Idaho."

Here are some very interesting town names.

Alabama- Aimwell, Bobo, Muck City

Alaska- Chicken, Deadhorse, Unalaska

Arizona- Bumble Bee, Goobertown, Why

Arkansas- Experiment, Fifty-Six, Okay

California- Deadman Crossing, Peanut, You Bet

Colorado- Dinosaur, Hygiene, No Name

Connecticut- Giants Neck, Hourglass, Cocked Hat

Florida- Christmas, Mayo, Weeki Wachee

Georgia- Between, Chickasawhatchee, Santa Clause

Idaho- Bliss, Butte, Slickpoo

Illinois- Fishhook, Normal, Roachtown

Indiana- Acme, Loogootee, Toad Hop

Iowa- Diagonal, Gravity, Manly

Kansas- Buttermilk, Hope, Rome

Kentucky- Do Stop, Monkey's Eyebrow

Louisiana- Belcher, Uncle Sam, Waterproof

Maine- Bald Head, Bath, Beans Corner Bingo

Maryland- Accident, Boring, Pomonkey

Massachusetts- Belchertown, Egypt, Sandwich

Michigan- Bad Axe, Paradise, Podunk

Minnesota- Blue Earth, Embarrass, Sleepy Eye

Mississippi- Alligator, Hot Coffee, Yazoo City

Missouri- Frankenstein, Pleasant Hope, Useful

Montana- Elmo, Hungry Horse, Yaak

Nebraska- Colon, Valentine, Worms

Nevada- Jackpot, Lost Nation, Sandwich Landing

New Jersey- Cheesequake, Egg Harbor, Love Ladies

New Mexico- Elephant Butte, Tingle, Truth or Consequences

New York- Cat Elbow Corner, Neversink, Yaphank

North Carolina- Big Lick, Duck, Welcome

North Dakota- Concrete, Hoople, Zap

Ohio- Blue Ball, Knockemstiff, Three Legs Town

Oklahoma- Cookietown, Happyland, Okay

Oregon- Boring, Half.com, Idiotville

Pennsylvania- Bird-in-Hand, Eighty-Four, Fear Not

Rhode Island- Quidnick, Quonochontaug, Woonsocket

South Carolina- Coward, Ninety Six, South of the Border

South Dakota- Hummer, Igloo, Red Shirt

Tennessee- Defeated, Nameless, Smartt (Not a Typo)

Texas- Cut-n-Shoot, Ding Dong, Hoop and Holler

Utah- Mexican Hat, Plain City, Notown

Virginia- Butts, Lick Skillet, Needmore

Washington- Index, Tumtum, Walla Walla

West Virginia- Big Ugly, HooHoo, Lost City

Wisconsin- Imalone, Ubet, Wanderoos

Wyoming- Chugwater, Cokeville, Muddy Gap

Weird Laws

There are some really stupid and weird laws out there. Here are some great ones.

Alabama: You can't open an umbrella on a street because it might scare horses. You can't drive the wrong way down one-way roads with a lantern on the front of your vehicle.

Alaska: Moose cannot be viewed from an airplane, or pushed out of an airplane. In Anchorage: you cannot tie a dog to the roof of your car. In Juneau, flamingo owners can't let their pet into a barbershop.

Arizona: You cannot hunt camels. When attacked by a criminal, you can only defend yourself with the same weapon the other person has.

Arkansas: In Fayetteville, you cannot kill any living creature.

California: Sunshine is guaranteed to the masses. It is a misdemeanor to shoot at any kind of game from a moving vehicle unless the target is a whale. No vehicle without a driver can exceed 60mph. In Arcadia, peacocks have the right of way on streets or driveways.

In Belvedere, there is a city council order that reads: "No dog shall be in a public place without its master on a leash."

Colorado: One may not mutilate a rock in a state park.

Connecticut: You can be stopped by police for biking over 65mph. Officially, to be a pickle it must bounce.

Delaware: It is illegal to fly over bodies of water without sufficient food or drink.

Florida: If an elephant is tied to a parking meter, a fee must be payed.

Hawaii: No billboards are allowed. Coins may not be in people's ears. Residents can be fined for not owning a boat.

Idaho: You cannot fish on a camel's back. In Boise, you cannot fish from a giraffe's neck.

Illinois: The English language is not to be spoken.

Kansas: Mules can't be used to hunt ducks.

Kentucky: You cannot dye a duckling blue and sell it unless 6 are for sale.

Louisiana: There is a $500 fine for instructing a pizza man to deliver a pizza to a friend without the friend knowing. Cannot shoot lasers at police.

Maine: You can't step out of a plane in flight. In South Berwick, it is illegal to park in front of a Dunkin' Donuts.

Maryland: In Rockville, it is illegal to remove a public building by writing on it.

Minnesota: It is illegal to stand around any building without a good reason.

Nevada: You cannot drive a camel on a highway.

Oklahoma also has some very interesting and weird laws just like many other states:

In Ada, you may be put in jail for wearing New York Jets clothing.

In Hawthorne, it is unlawful to put a person that is hypnotized in a display window.

In Bartlesville, nobody can have more than two adult cats.

In Yukon, it is illegal for a horse to be tied in front of city hall.

In Wynona, mules can't drink water from bird baths.

In Oklahoma City, you may not eat a hamburger while walking backward downtown.

In Bartlesville, people may not play catch on a street.

In Yukon, you must honk your horn while passing another vehicle.

In Clinton, if you lean against a public building, you will be fined.

In Oklahoma City, the mayor is not allowed to go on strike.

Like many other states, *Washington* has weird laws. Here are some of the most interesting ones I found.

Lollipops are banned throughout all of Washington.

TV's cannot be bought on Sundays in Spokane.

You're not allowed to ride an ugly horse in Wilbur.

It is illegal to paint polka dots on the American Flag throughout all of Washington.

You're not allowed to dance and drink in the same place in Lyndon.

It is illegal to kneel on a pedestrian sidewalk in Spokane.

You are not allowed to walk outside if you have the common cold throughout all of Washington.

You cannot buy a mattress on Sunday in all of Washington.

It is illegal to pretend your parents are rich in Washington.

You cannot wear a life jacket near the Spokane River in Spokane.

If you're a motorist with criminal intentions, you must stop at the city limits and alert the chief of police before entering town.

It is illegal to destroy the beer cask or beer bottle of another person in Washington.

In Seattle, it is illegal to bring a fishbowl on a bus because the sloshing water might disturb others.

Weird Phobias

Boo - Totally weird, but real phobias:

Hippopotomonstrosesquipedaliophobia:

Fear of long words

Chometophobia:

Fear of cash or money

Arachibutyrophobia:

Fear of peanut butter sticking to the roof of one's mouth

Francophobia:

Fear of anything relating to France

Heliophobia:

Fear of the sun

Heminthephobia:

Fear of being infested with worms

Hydrophobia:

Fear of water or liquids

Lutraphobia:

Fear of otters

Anglephobia:

Fear of England

Areomoliorphobia:

Fear of going to the bathroom on a plane

Tetraphobia:

Fear of the number 4

Spectrophobia:

Fear of one's own reflection

Phobophobia

Fear of having a phobia (F.D.R. WIN)

Weird Stuff Sold on Ebay

You would not believe how many weird things have been sold on eBay. Here are just a few.

Ghost in a Jar - $50,922

Virgin Mary Grilled Cheese Sandwich - $28,000

Ex-Wife's Wedding Dress - $3,850

Vampire Killing Kit - $2,005.50

John F. Kennedy Assassination Shooter's Perch Window - $3,001,501

Doritos Cheese Pope Hat - $1,209

Twenty-Six Shrunken Heads - $25

UFO Detector - $135

Russian Test Space Shuttle - Bidding topped out at $25,200

Serial Killer's Fingernails - $9.99

Dumb, Dumber, and Dumbest

Dumb Warnings

There are some really stupid warnings out there. Here are a few great ones.

An unknown air conditioner says: "Caution: Avoid dropping air conditioners out of windows."

An unknown blow dryer says: "Warning: Do not use while sleeping."

The White-Westinghouse 1600 Blow Dryer states: "Keep away from water."

The Rowenta Iron states: "Warning: Never iron clothes on body."

An unknown vacuum cleaner says: "Do not use to pick up gasoline or flammable liquids. Do not use to pick up anything that is currently burning."

A Child-Sized Superman Costume says: "Wearing of this garment does not enable you to fly."

A Batman Costume says: Warning: "Cape does not enable user to fly."

A Graduation Gown says: “Do not wash or dry clean.”

A Power Puff Girls Halloween Costume states: “You cannot save the world!”

Ray-Ban Sunglasses say: “It is not suitable for driving under conditions of poor light.”

Miller Light says: “Consumption of alcoholic beverages impairs your ability to drive a car or operate machinery, and may cause health problems.”

McDonalds coffee states: “Warning-contents may be hot!”

Tesco Fruit Juice cartons say(on the bottom): “Keep upright.”

Sainsbury Mineral Water states: “Suitable for vegetarians.”

Silk Soy Milk says: “Shake well and buy often.”

Moet White Star Champagne states: “Warning: Remove label before placing in microwave.”

Various Computers say: “Keyboard not detected. Press F1 to continue.”

Various personal computers state(on startup): “No keyboard detected. Press any key to continue.”

An unknown European camera: "This camera will only work when film is inside."

An unknown Minidisc Player states: "Best when used with Minidisc recorders and players."

Hungry Jack Lite Syrup states after a long description of how to heat the bottle: "Syrup bottle may be hot!"

Fritos state: "You could be a winner! No purchase necessary. Details inside."

American Airlines Peanuts used to say: "Instructions: Open packet, eat peanuts."

Marks and Spencer Bread Pudding says: "Product will be hot after heating."

Tesco's Tiramisu dessert says(on bottom): "Do not turn upside down."

Sainsbury Peanuts state: "Warning: This product contains nuts."

Nabisco Easy Cheese says: "For best results, remove cap."

An unknown hair coloring states: "Do not use as an ice cream topping."

Ciba Vision Pure Eyes says: "Use before expiration date."

An unknown Christmas lights package states: "Warning: For indoor or outdoor use only."

An unknown fire extinguisher says: "Caution: Non-flammable."

An unknown mattress states: "Warning: Do not attempt to swallow."

A Clemenson, SC road states: Caution: "Water on road during rain."

Rim Drive, Durango, Colorado states: "Warning: Do not hit this sign."

Highway 26, Idaho Falls, Idaho states: "Warning to tourists: don't laugh at natives."

A Harry Potter Toy Broom says: "This broom does not actually fly."

An unknown 500-piece puzzle states: "Some assembly required."

An unknown Beach Ball says: "CAUTION: This is not a life saving device."

Dumb Crooks

If I ever become a victim of house invasion, I would want it robbed by a dumb crook. The stupidity of these crooks is just hilarious. Here are a few great stories.

People are advised to now pick up hitchhikers. After robbing a bank, a criminal decided to hitchhike. He flagged down a ride, and asked the person to drive him home. However, the criminal's driver was an undercover cop. Instead of getting a ride home, that criminal got a ride to a police station. Next time, the criminal should rob a car first.

A not so bright criminal chose a bank to rob. However, his weapon of choice was his index finger. When the robber barged into the bank with his index finger held out, he demanded money. The teller told the criminal to wait. Instead of waiting longer, the criminal went to another nearby bank. The criminal entered the bank, leapt on the counter and tried wrestling a key from the teller. The teller was stronger than the robber though. The teller told the robber to "Get out of here" and so the robber left. Police arrived shortly after the teller at the first bank called them. The criminal was soon arrested after being found in nearby bushes outside the second bank.

Is this robbery a coincidence? A criminal tried to rob the same store as before. What makes this robbery creepy is the criminal broke the same window, stole much of the same merchandise, and was even seen by the same witness as before. So the witness had no problem identifying the robber for the police.

This is one of the stupidest criminals ever. First, this criminal smashed his fist through a window in a shed, which shredded his hand. He then broke into a second story nearby garage. But he forgot his flashlight and it's dark. So he didn't see the hole in the floor, and fell through it. Then he finds himself in the first story garage, where he fell into a grease pit and cracks his cranium. He then decided his best course of action was to break into the house itself. So he shattered a front door window and broke in. He slowly crept in, and fell down the cellar stairs. The crook finally realized that today wasn't his lucky day. So he left and got in his car. He drove downhill and lost control. He smashed into a tree and his already injured head hit the steering wheel. He then got out of his car and locked it. Then for some reason he retraced his fall into the grease pit. He then staggered out of the garage and decided to go home. Unfortunately for him, he couldn't find his car keys. The crook then smashed his car's rear window, climbed over the backseat, and broke the gearshift, setting the car into neutral. The car slowly rolled downhill. The criminal jumpstarted the car, but couldn't unlock the steering wheel. He then crashed into a second tree. With the third blow to his head he lost consciousness. His head then fell against the steering wheel, setting off the car horn, and alerting the nearby neighbors, who called the cops. The criminal was soon arrested. No wonder the cops called him the "Bad Luck Burglar."

Two robbers were trying in vain to open a safe at a local grocery store in Larch Barrens, Maryland. An hour had gone by, giving police plenty of time to arrive at the scene. Apparently the laser the robbers were using was a battery operated laser tag gun from a local amusement park.

A convicted criminal was being escorted to jail. He escaped, but in the effort of escaping his feet were cut and bleeding badly. A while later, the cops got a call from a local hospital. On the standard hospital forms, a patient had filled out for injury “Escape from jail.”

A man thought it would be a good idea to rob a bank. He had almost everything he needed. What did he forget? His brain. When he went to the bank, he didn’t realize it was pay day for the FBI in the area. So when he demanded money, he heard several guns clicking behind him. Along with multiple shackles.

A man entered a hotel. He decided to rob an elderly man walking out of the restroom. However, the man was once a sheriff, and knew what to yell for help. Several other sheriffs came to his aid, and the robber was soon in shackles. The robber must not have had good eyesight, because outside of the hotel was a big sign saying “State Sheriff Convention.”

A man robbed a house. However he made one mistake that would lead the police to him and the robber to jail.

At the scene of the crime the robber had left his cell phone. The stupid crook even had pictures of himself on it. With the help of the pictures, the crook was easily tracked down and put into his rightful place: A prison cell.

Many robbers need more education and schooling. A robber at a bank passed a note to the teller demanding money. The teller said he could not read it, so the robber tried to rewrite it. While the dumb crook was rewriting the note, the teller took a step back without the crook noticing and activated a silent alarm. Perhaps there's a school in prison for this crook....

Dumb Quotes

We have all said some dumb things in our lifetime, but no one was around to hear us.

These popular quotes showcase some of the moments where celebrities weren't thinking much about what they were saying...

“The world is more like it is now than it ever was before”- Dwight Eisenhower

“Solutions are not the answer”- Richard Nixon

“They misunderestimated me”- George W. Bush

“I’m a very spontaneous person, so I’m always thinking about what I’m going to do next”- Miss Teen West Virginia

“The word ‘genius’ isn’t applicable in football. A genius is a guy like Norman Einstein”- Joe Theisman

“Most of my clichés aren’t original”- Chuck Knox

“If your parents never had children, chances are you won’t either”- Dick Cavett

“If we don’t succeed, we run the risk of failure”- Dan Quayle, former US VP

“Smoking kills. If you’re killed, you lose a very important part of your life.”-Brooke Shields

“And now, the sequence of events in no particular order”-Dan Rather

“For NASA, space is still a high priority”- Dan Quayle

“Comedy is funny”- Goldie Hawn

"You can hardly tell where the computer models finish and the real dinosaurs begin"- Laura Dern on Jurassic Park

"For most people, death comes at the end of their lives"- GLR radio broadcaster.

"If history repeats itself, I think we should expect the same thing again"- Terry Venables, former football player

"I invented the internet"- Al Gore

"It is wonderful to be here in the great state of Chicago"- Dan Quayle

Q: If you could live forever, would you, and why? A: "I would not live forever, because we shouldn't live forever, because if we were supposed to live forever, than we would live forever, but we cannot live forever, which is why I would not live forever"- Miss Alabama 1994

"Congratulations on breaking my record. I always thought the record would stand until it was broken"- Yogi Berra, Former baseball player

"We don't necessarily discriminate. We just exclude certain types of people"- Colonel Gerald Wellman

“If only faces could talk”- Pat Summerall

“I don’t diet. I just don’t eat as much as I’d like to”- Linda Evangelista, model

“The streets are safe in Philadelphia. It’s the people who make them unsafe”- Mayor Frank Rizzo

“I can not tell you how grateful I am. I am filled with humidity”- Gib Lewis, political consultant

“A bachelor’s life is no life for a single man”- Samuel Goldwyn, Film Producer

“In the long run, the answer to unemployment is to create more jobs”-George W. Bush

Unique People, Places, and Things

Before They Were Famous

Ever wonder if you are related to someone famous? Well, many famous people changed their names. Now here is your chance to find out.

Albert Brooks - Albert Lawrence Einstein

Alicia Keys - Alicia Augello Cook

Bob Dylan - Robert Zimmermur

Cher - Cherilyn Sarkisian

Buddy Holly - Charles Hardin Holley

Chuck Norris - Carlos Ray

David Bowie - David Robert Jones

Elton John - Reginald Kenneth Dwight

Elvis Costello - Declan Patrick Aloysius McManus

Fred Astaire - Frederick Austerlitz

George Orwell - Eric Arthur Blair

Ginger Rogers - Virginia Katherine McMath

Groucho Marx - Julius Henry Marx

Harry Houdini - Ehrich Weiss

Jerry Lewis - Joseph Levitch

Judy Garland - Frances Gumm

Mariah Carey - Maria Nunez

Marilyn Monroe - Norma Jean Mortenson

Mark Twain - Samuel Langhorne Clemers

Mel Brooks - Melvin Kaminsky

Mother Teresa - Agnes Gonyha Bojaxhiu

Mr. T - Lawrence Tero

Nicolas Cage - Nicolas Coppola

P!nk - Alecia Moore

Ray Charles - Ray Charles Robinson

Ringo Starr - Richard Starkey

Stevie Wonder - Steveland Morris

Tina Turner - Anna Mae Bullock

Vanilla Ice - Robert Van Winkle

Whoopie Goldberg - Caryn Johnson

Disney

The "Happiest Place on Earth" is the second most visited place in the United States. But here are some facts you might not have known.

- Over 40 square miles, Walt Disney World Resort is about as big as San Francisco.
- Wash and dry a load of laundry every day for 52 years. That's how much the staff at Disney does every day.
- More than 75 million cokes are consumed ever year at Disney, while 13 million bottles of water are drunk every year.
- At Disney World, every year 300,000 pounds of popcorn are eaten.
- If all the autograph books sold at Disney annually were stacked, they would be the height of 200 Cinderella Castles.
- Princess autograph books? End to end; they would reach 88 miles into space.
- According to lost-and-found staffers, a glass eye was turned in and claimed.

- Lost and found at Disney Parks finds:

  - An average of 210 pairs of sunglasses a day.

  -6,000 cell phones a year.

  -3,500 digital cameras a year.

  -1,800 hats a year.

  -7,500 autograph books a year.

- There are no stones in the Cinderella Castle. The shell of the building is made of fiberglass.
- The Earffel Tower, Disney's Hollywood Studios water tower, would wear a hat size 342 and ¾.
- If you wanted to stay in all the guest rooms in all the hotels and resorts in Disney World Resort property, at one room a night, it would take more than 68 years.
- When walking from Canada Pavilion to Mexico Pavilion in Walt Disney World's EPCOT, you cover over 1 and ½ miles.
- Walt Disney World only closed its doors once. Why? Because of Hurricane Floyd. When? September 14th to September 16th in 1999.

- Disney World Resort is the biggest on-site employer in the U.S.A.
- The pavements at EPCOT are painted a certain shade of pink, which makes the grass look greener.
- The Tower of Terror is 199 feet tall. If it were one foot taller, Disney Parks would have to put an airplane signal on top of it.
- When the Tower of Terror was being built, it was struck by lightning.
- Now let us travel from East to West and have a look at Disney Land:
- The oldest tree in Disney Land is a two feet tall pine growing in Gepetto's village in Storybook land. It is over 150 years old.
- Before the Disney Hotel opened in 1955, there were less than 100 hotel rooms available in Anaheim.
- Ever been on Space Mountain? Look closely the next time, and you'll see some of the asteroids flying overhead are really oversized chocolate chip cookies.

- Main Street is set for 1910. Tomorrow land is set in 1986. Why these years? Because they are the years of Hailey's Comet.
- The trashcans at the Disney parks are no more than 25 paces apart.
- Before there was Mickey Mouse, There was Oswald the Lucky Rabbit.
- Walt Disney only attended one year of high school.
- Walt Disney's favorite meal was chili and beans.
- Walt Disney won more Oscars than anyone else.
- Walt Disney was dyslexic.

Kiwi Birds

The kiwi bird is a majestic flightless bird. It is very rare to see one but when you do you will love them. They are a brown gray color and very fat. They are an endangered species and we should really try to save them and conserve their habitat.

Kiwi Bird Facts:

- They are only 9 inches in length.
- Kiwi Birds only live in New Zealand.
- They are nocturnal.
- Their diet consists of berries, bugs, and grubs that are underground which is why they have such long beaks.
- Their main predators are dogs.
- Even though they are the size of a chicken they lay eggs the size of an ostrich.
- Five different species of the kiwi bird are around: The Brown Kiwi's, Little Spotted Kiwi, Great Spotted Kiwi, North Island Brown Kiwi , and the Rowi.
- The Rowi Kiwi is the rarest.
- Their beaks have vibrations to detect insects moving underground.
- They are the National Bird of New Zealand.
- Kiwis are the only birds with nostrils on the end of their beaks.
- They are flightless.

- A female kiwi bird is larger than the males.
- They live in burrows underground.
- The male kiwis sit on the egg.
- They have no tail and two inch wings.
- They are very aggressive and defensive. If they see or hear another kiwi bird come onto its territory it will attack it.
- Female kiwis lay around 3 eggs each season in all different nests.
- Only around 800 kiwi birds are left in the wild which is why we need to protect their habitat.
- The kiwi bird's fur is coarse and hair-like.
- The wide spacing of their claws helps them run up to 30 miles per hour.
- They got their name by their distinct call which sounds like "keeee-weee keeee-weee".
- The largest kind of kiwi bird is the Great Spotted Kiwi .

Koalas

Hope you will enjoy these facts of koalas I have collected for you!

- Most koalas in the world are nocturnal.
- They spend up to 20 hours a day sleeping or resting.
- In 1920 nearly eight million koalas were killed.
- Baby koalas are referred as joeys.
- They are generally silent but communicate with growls, grunts, and loud bellows.
- Koalas receive over 90% of their fluid intake from eucalyptus leaves.
- They only drink water when they are ill or when there is not enough moisture in the eucalyptus leaves.
- The word koala in Aboriginal language is thought to mean 'does not drink'.
- Koalas live up to 12-20 years if in captivity.
- Hunters kill koalas for their soft and smooth fur.

- Koalas are not bears but marsupials.
- There are probably 2,000-8,000 koalas left in the world.
- They spend 4 hours of every night eating.
- They can eat 1 pound of leaves a day.
- Joeys live in their mothers pouch for 6-7 months; they then leave the pouch and cling to their mother's back.
- They grow up to be 16-32 inches long and 9-33 pounds.
- Koalas seem to have 2 thumbs on each hand.

Koala Stories

In 1980 a koala named Cuthbert from a colony near Melbourne became attracted to the noise of a motorbike and eventually took the occasional ride on it, seated on the pillion and holding firmly on to the machine's owner.

It seems that koalas have a taste for money. In 1983, a koala named Clinker was present at a ceremony at the Royal Botanic Gardens in Sydney, when the Kimberly Clark industrial group presented a check for 50,000 Australian dollars to the World Wildlife Fund. The company made the mistake of using a gimmick: the check was printed on a eucalyptus leaf. Clinker could think of better uses for it than banking it. He seized it and ate it.

There is an unlikely story that a koala found its way to Scotland with a sailor in the early 1800s, and was returned to Australia at the end of the visit. The first authenticated instance of a koala leaving its native land was in 1880, when London Zoo in Regent's Park acquired one. It was given very special care, but sadly it lived for only 14 months. One night, it fell into a washstand and suffocated to death.

Unusual Deaths

These are some of the most unusual deaths you will ever hear, I hope you're ready though, because here we go....

In December 1999, a man died after falling off the roof of his car. He was apparently arguing with his girlfriend during a drive home along Interstate 88. Although the vehicle was traveling over 65 mph in the midst of gale-force winds, the man decided to exit the car onto the roof, presumably to escape from the fight. The man fell to the ground and was rushed to the hospital but died the next day due to head injuries. The woman driving was charged with a DWI.

A handicapped man, annoyed that an elevator closed and departed without him, thinks it over before ramming his wheelchair into the door not 1, 2 but 3 times, only to fall down the elevator shaft and plunge to his death.

A lawyer testing the safety of the windows in a skyscraper in downtown Toronto, Canada crashed through a window and fell 24 floors down to his demise.

A fisherman in Kiev, Ukraine electrocuted himself while fishing in the river Tereblya. The 43 year old man connected cables to the main power supply of his house, and trailed the end into the river. The electric shock killed the fish, and he then waded in to collect his catch, but neglected to remove the live wire, and ultimately suffered the same fate as the fish. Ironically, the man was fishing for a mourning meal to commemorate the 1st anniversary of his mother in law's death.

Humberto Hernandez, a 24 year old Oakland, California resident, was killed from being struck in the face by an airborne fire hydrant while walking on a sidewalk; a passing car blew a tire and swerved onto the sidewalk, striking the fire hydrant. The force of the water pressure shot the 200-pound hydrant at Hernandez with enough force to kill him.

Gregory Biggs, a homeless man in Fort Worth, Texas was hit by a car being driven by Chante Jawan Mallard, who had been drinking and taking drugs that night. Biggs' torso became lodged in Mallard's windshield with severe but not immediately fatal injuries. Mallard drove home and left the car in her garage with Biggs still lodged in her car's windshield. She repeatedly visited Biggs and even apologized for hitting him. Biggs died of his injuries several hours later. Chante Mallard was tried and convicted for murder in this case and received a 50-year prison sentence.

Walter Hallas, a 26-year-old store clerk in Leeds, England, was so afraid of dentists that in 1979 he asked a fellow worker to try to cure his toothache by punching him in the jaw. The punch caused Hallas to fall down, hitting his head, and he died of a fractured skull.

A man hit by a car in New York in 1977 got up uninjured, but lay back down in front of the car when a bystander told him to pretend he was hurt so he could collect insurance money. The car rolled forward and crushed him to death.

Robert Gary Jones, 38, was jogging and listening to his iPod when he was hit from behind and killed by a small plane making an emergency landing on a South Carolina beach.

Vladimir Ladyzhensky, a competitor from Russia, died while participating in the World Sauna Championships (Yes, it's real) in Finland, after he had spent 6 minutes in a sauna that had been heated up to 110 degrees Celsius (230 degrees Fahrenheit). The other finalist, a 5-time champion Timo Kaukonen, was taken to the hospital after suffering from serious burns on his body. Because of this incident, no further World Sauna Championships will be held.

Timothy Treadwell, an American environmentalist who had lived in the wilderness among bears for thirteen summers in a remote region in Alaska, and his girlfriend Amie Huguenard were killed and partially consumed by a bear. An audio recording of their deaths was captured on a video camera which had been turned on at the beginning of the incident.

Phillip Quinn, a 24-year-old American from Kent, Washington was killed during an attempt to heat up a lava lamp bulb on his kitchen stove while observing it from a few feet away. The heat built up pressure in the bulb until it exploded, spraying shards of glass. One pierced his heart, killing him. The circumstances of his death were later repeated and confirmed in a 2006 episode of the popular science television series MythBusters.

Every player on the Basanga soccer team was killed during a game in the Democratic Republic of Congo. The field was struck by a fork bolt of lightning, hitting and killing the entire team instantly. Nobody on the opposing team was struck by the bolt.

A dance teacher tangoed to his death straight out of the fifth floor of his dance studio. How, you may ask? He was apparently demonstrating how to keep the head high while dancing by looking at the ceiling. Would you take that advice next time?

One early morning (3am, to be exact) a man died after hitting a ski lift tower while riding down the slope on a sled made out of yellow foam. The man and his friends had, apparently, hiked up a ski run called Stump Alley and undid some of yellow foam protectors on the lift towers, which are used to protect the skiers who might hit the towers. The man hit one of the towers he had stolen the pads off of, and died.

Ever think you may play just a little to much video games? Well, you've never played as much as these guys:

In 1981, a 19 year old man named Jeff Dailey became the first known person to die while playing video games. After beating the high score on an arcade game named Berserk, he succumbed to a massive heart attack and died. 1 year later, the same thing happened to an 18 year old on the SAME game.

Lee Seung Seop, a 28 year old South Korean, collapsed and died of fatigue in 2005 after playing the popular computer game Starcraft for almost 50 consecutive hours in an internet café.

Emoticons

The History of :-)

The first recorded electronic emoticon was created on the 19th of September, 1982, at 11:44, by a man named Dr. Scott Fahlman, of the Carnegie Mellon University in Pittsburg, Tennessee.

Even though Fahlman was credited of being the inventor of :-) & :-(, he wasn't the first. In 1967, a Reader's Digest article showed a similar "smiley" to Fahlman's.

The first yellow smiley face though came much earlier -- almost two decades to be exact. It was created by Harvey Ball in 1963 for an insurance company to raise employee and customer morale. This yellow smiley face has now become a worldwide phenomenon, appearing on buttons, T-Shirts, and on the internet a plenty. The yellow smiley is so popular, a international holiday has been made for it.

Some even say the smiley was used even before 1963! One decade earlier, in 1953, the movie "Lili" premiered, with a movie poster for the movie had three different emoticon-looking faces, each with its own emotion.

Now, with the invention of instant messaging, you may have a little smile, frown, or tear, in every message, and of course a nose and some eyes to go with it!

FrankenSmiley

Combine any of the following pieces to make your own smiley face, in the comfort of your own home.

(All emoticon parts facing --> way)

Eyes - (with or without eyebrows)

: >: B = 8 ; O; O: }: }; X

Nose

- ~ >

Mouth

) (O] } \ P / > < 0 # |

D C { [ )~ (~

ALIEN SIGHTINGS

A man lived in a small town called Chatsworth, in northwest Georgia. He was just outside, was walking around enjoying the clear night and saw this bright light. He thought it was a star until it started to move. He had never seen a plane or anything move like that. It would go from side to side covering at least 2 miles in the blink of an eye. Then it would go up and down just as far and as fast. It would be there one sec and gone the next and then back again. It was a bright white light, and then it would pulsate blue, green and a red color. He was still in shock, he couldn't get a photo but he saw it and no one would believe him.

A couple of months ago, a man and his brother were riding bicycles. It was night and he looked into the sky and noticed a bright circular object. At first, he thought it was the wishing star. He couldn't take his eyes off of it because it was 3 times bigger then what the wishing star usually was. He remembers telling his brother to look, he saw it too. Then it just disappeared right in front of his eyes. The object got smaller and smaller till it was gone, as if it faded away.

Months after that, he saw the same thing happening while he was driving to school; however, It was day time. He kept trying to convince himself that it was an airplane, but it wasn't moving, and it was a circular bright like object like he had seen that night months ago, then it also has disappeared.

The next night, as he was driving from his cousin's house, he kept glancing up at the stars. His two younger brothers were with him. As he continued to look, he saw something go across the sky. It was a radiant blue ball with a golden trail; it was bright and big too. He got so freaked out by it that he slammed on the breaks, scaring his brothers too. The brother was in front seat looked up just in time to see the object go over the trees, and then it was gone. His brother in the back didn't see it, but he said he had seen the bright blue lights.

He was waiting in the parking lot of Clifford's Dining Hall for a tow truck to come and pick up his car which had just blown a water pump. His brother-in-law was keeping him company. While waiting, he reclined on the hood of the car and was looking at the stars, and specifically admiring the Big Dipper.

He caught movement out of his eye and looked slightly below, and to the right of the Big Dipper, and saw three triangular shapes in a very tight triangular formation. They were moving from east to west across the sky. He wasn't sure at first that he was seeing this, so he asked his brother-in-law to look in the sky. By this time, the three triangular shapes were to the left of the Big Dipper, but still below it. He immediately spotted them as well. They appeared to be heading in a straight line, and were moving incredibly fast. In less than 30 seconds, they were out of sight. The weird part was that these three craft didn't make any noise at all. They were clearly about a mile north of the westerly approach of landing aircraft, and in fact saw many jets that evening coming in to land at Mitchell International

Airport, which is located about 8 miles east of our location. These triangular shapes were definitely not commercial aircraft. They appeared to have some kind of texture to their forms, but he was unable to determine with his naked eye what the textures might have been. Since there was nothing higher or lower than these shapes, he had no idea of them since due to a lack of reference point. They did appear to be uniform in appearance.

Three men were sitting on the front porch of their father's apartment for a family get together. They were eating dinner when suddenly a large, completely circular object shot slowly through the air. Dad yelled for his son to get the video recorder. He grabbed it, and recorded it as it then rose higher and higher into the atmosphere. It had three red lights on its bottom, and one yellowish green light on top. The UFO was no aircraft they've ever heard of before when it gave off a high pitched ringing sound.

A group of teenagers after a night of movies and pizza decided to go for a walk. By this time it was around 1:30 in the morning. A lot of them were energetic and running around until they stopped and saw a red streak in the sky. It disappeared quickly. Shortly after, over the hills near them they saw alternating white lights moving left to right getting brighter then fading lighter. This repeated itself for some time. They were so psyched but, they didn't get a chance to film it. They believe it was a UFO because the lights were moving way too fast and absolutely too bright. No matter what the memory still remains.

There is a person who never believed in aliens until about a year ago. What happened was that he was out hunting for rabbits and his father was back at the truck fishing a little bit. He'd been out for a few hours and was coming back to camp. When he looked up and followed a little bird across the sky and in the background he saw what looked like an airplane at first. It was long and silvery metallic it seemed. It looked like one of those funny planes with the nose bent down, a "Concorde" he thought they called it, but it looked funny because his city of San Angelo, Texas doesn't have a big enough airport for a plane that size. It didn't take him long to realize though that this thing wasn't moving at all. It was just sort of stationary and was pretty far off so he couldn't verify that it wasn't making any noise. He started off on a quick pace to tell his dad to look at this thing but he was a ways off that it would take him a bit to get there. So as he was moving along this thing just seemed to disappear. Not so much as it shot off but like it just blended in with the sky. Like a chameleon only it was invisible altogether. When he watched this happen he became very frightened and started to run as fast as he could to the camp so his father and he can leave as soon as possible.

The first alien abduction story that made news was that of Betty and Barney Hill. On September 19, 1961, they were driving to Portsmouth when they saw a bright light in the sky. Soon, some human-like figures got out from a disk-like craft and approached the Hills. The human-like figures with their vehicle began hovering over the Hills' car. The aliens soon abducted them. The Hills later claimed to have entered a state of altered consciousness during the abduction.

Another famous alien abduction story is that of Villa Boas. Antonio Villas Boas was a Brazilian farmer who was working at night, when he saw a red star in the night sky. It was actually an egg-shaped craft with red light. He began attempting to flee from the scary object that seemed to be approaching him. But he was soon captivated by a humanoid. The humanoid, as described by Boas, had blue eyes and made sounds like barks and yelps. Three other human-like beings grabbed Boas and took him to their craft. Inside the craft, his clothes were stripped off to cover him with jelly. Later the abductors performed a blood examination on Boas and then left him in a room in accompaniment of a female who resembled the other humanoid figures. Boas claims to have fallen ill when in captivity. When he returned to Earth, he realized that he had been abducted for four hours. This was truly a very scary alien abduction.

Another scary alien abduction took place on Dechmont Law, a hill outside Livingston, Scotland. Bob Taylor, a forestry worker encountered an unidentified object, which dragged him along the ground. Investigators found some strange-looking marks on the ground. This is the strangest discovery in Scotland yet.

EXPENSIVE STUFF

Most Expensive and Valuable Sports Stuff

At Super Bowl XLII, in which the New York Giants and the New England Patriots faced off, the tickets were between $700 and $900 apiece.

Most Expensive Sports to Play- #1-Yacht Racing #2-Vintage Auto Racing #3-Polo #4-Aerobatics #5-Golf

The Most Valuable Sports Franchises are- #1-Manchester United (Soccer) #2-Dallas Cowboys (Football) #3-New York Yankees (Baseball) #4-Washington Redskins (Football) #5-New England Patriots (Football)

The Most Valuable Athletes are- #1-Tiger Woods (Golf) #2-Floyd Mayweather (Boxing) #3-Kobe Bryant (Basketball) #4-Phil Mickelson (Golf) #5-David Beckham (Soccer)

The most expensive baseball card is a 1909 Honus Wagner tobacco card. It was formerly owned by Wayne Gretzky. He sold it for $2.35 million.

The Most Expensive Random Stuff

The most expensive video game console in the world is the Nintendo Wii Supreme. Why? Because it is coated in 2.5 kg of 22k gold. The front buttons are decorated with 78 quarter-cut diamonds weighing in at 19.5 carats. It is $481,250.

The Bugatti Veyron is the most expensive car in world. It is estimated to be at $2.3million.

The most expensive TV in the world is the Prestige HD Supreme Rose. It is worth $2.3 million.

The most expensive house in the world is a 27-story skyscraper in India. India's richest man built the house for $1 billion. It has a private health club, gym, dance studio, ballroom, fifty-seat screening room, three helipads, an elevated garden, and an underground parking for one hundred-sixty vehicles.

THE SUPER BOWL

The Super Bowl has had a great history and always will. Here are some interesting things about the NFL Championship.

On Super Bowl Sunday, there are fewer weddings than on any other day of the year.

In the 2004 Super Bowl halftime show, Janet Jackson had a revealing "wardrobe malfunction". That led to "Janet Jackson" being the most searched term on Google of all time.

On the first Super Bowl, the stadium was almost half empty.

Americans eat more food on Super Bowl Sunday than on any other day, except Thanksgiving.

Lamar Hunt, Kansas City Chief's owner, came up with the name "Super Bowl". He named it after his child's favorite play toy, the Super Ball.

Super Bowl Winners

1967- Green Bay Packers

1968- Green Bay Packers

1969- New York Jets

1970- Kansas City Chiefs

1971- Baltimore Colts

1972- Dallas Cowboys

1973- Miami Dolphins

1974- Miami Dolphins

1975- Pittsburgh Steelers

1976- Pittsburgh Steelers

1977- Oakland Raiders

1978- Dallas Cowboys

1979- Pittsburgh Steelers

1980- Pittsburgh Steelers

1981- Oakland Raiders

1982- San Francisco 49ers

1983- Washington Redskins

1984- Los Angeles Raiders

1985- San Francisco 49ers

1986- Chicago Bears

1987- New York Giants

1988- Washington Redskins

1989- San Francisco 49ers

1990- San Francisco 49ers

1991- New York Giants

1992- Washington Redskins

1993- Dallas Cowboys

1994- Dallas Cowboys

1995- San Fransisco 49ers

1996- Dallas Cowboys

1997- Green Bay Packers

1998- Denver Broncos

1999- Denver Broncos

2000- St. Louis Rams

2001- Baltimore Ravens

2002- New England Patriots

2003- Tampa Bay Buccaneers

2004- New England Patriots

2005- New England Patriots

2006- Pittsburgh Steelers

2007- Indianapolis Colts

2008- New York Giants

2009- Pittsburgh Steelers

2010- New Orleans Saints

Mrs. Morrell's

Birthdays and Quotes

Who Shares Your Day?

What Did They Say?

Birthdays are important milestones. Everyone shares their special day with hundreds of others. Often those individuals have something memorable to say.

The following selection of birthdays and quotations are taken from the book Who Shares Your Day? What Did They Say? by Karen Morrell to be released in 2011.

Names, dates, and quotes were researched through a variety of sources and every effort has been made to substantiate accuracy. Years of birth, occupations, and birth names are provided. Individuals are listed in birth order and include actors, actresses, politicians, musicians, scientists, artists, mathematicians, authors, athletes, and dozens more.

These particular eight dates were chosen because each belongs to one of the co-authors of this book.

So, Maya, Nikki, Gabe, Brad, Henry, Josh, Gustavo, and Nick, let's see who shares your birthday and explore the unique messages they have for you!

February 28

People Who Have Something to Say – Feb 28

Michel deMontaigne – 1533 – French Philosopher and Writer

"My life has been full of terrible misfortunes most of which never happened."

Berthold Auerbach – 1812 – German Novelist

"Music washes away from the soul the dust of everyday life."

Marcel Pagnol – 1895 – French Writer, Producer, and Director

"The reason people find it so hard to be happy is that they always see the past better than it was, the present worse than it is, and the future less resolved than it will be."

Linus Pauling – 1901 – Scientist, Chemist, and Author

"The way to get good ideas is to get lots of ideas, and throw the bad ones away."

Tommy Tune – 1939 – Choreographer, Singer, Director, and Producer

"I like a show to unfold and keep presenting itself, surprising you."

Mario Andretti – 1940 – Race Car Driver

"Circumstances may cause interruption and delays, but never lose sight of your goal."

Bubba Smith – 1945 – Actor and Professional Athlete (Charles Aaron Smith)

"The ninth grade. I went from 5'9" to 6'8"."

Stephanie Beacham – 1947 – British Actress

"As far as my work is concerned, I see no impediment, and various advantages, to being deaf."

Bernadette Peters – 1948 – Actress and Singer (Bernadette Lazzara)

“You've gotta be original, because if you're like someone else, what do they need you for?”

Lemony Snicket – 1970 – Author (Daniel Handler)

“The only trouble I should get in for my writing is the trouble I make myself.”

Eric Lindros – 1973 – Professional Hockey Player

“It's not necessarily the amount of time you spend at practice that counts; it's what you put into the practice.”

Ali Larter – 1976 – Actress

“I don't care how stylish something is if it doesn't flatter me.”

Others Who Share Your Day – Feb 28

Florian Cajori – 1859 – Historian

Vincente Minnelli – 1903 – Film and Stage Director

Bugsy Siegel – 1906 – Gangster (Benjamin Siegel)

Barton Hepburn – 1906 – Actor

Milton Caniff – 1907 – Cartoonist

Earl Scheib – 1908 – Businessman

Zero Mostel – 1915 – Actor (Samuel Joel Mostel)

Lee Castle – 1915 – Musician, Trumpeter, and Bandleader

Peter Medawar – 1915 – Biologist

Audley Bowdler Williamson – 1916 – Manufacturer of Skin-care Products

Charles Durning – 1923 – Actor

Chris Craft – 1924 – Engineer

Leon N. Cooper – 1930 – Physicist

Gavin MacLeod – 1930 – Actor

Daniel C. Tsui – 1939 – Physicist

Joe South – 1940 – Musician and Singer (Joseph Alfred Souter)

Frank Bonner – 1942 – Actor

Charles Bernstein – 1943 – Composer of Music for TV and Films

Steven Cho – 1948 – Physicist

William Finn – 1952 – Film and Musical Composer and Lyricist

Paul Krugman – 1953 – Columnist

Jean Bourgain – 1954 – Mathematician

Gilbert Gottfried – 1955 – Actor

Ainsley Harriott – 1957 – British Celebrity Chef and Presenter

Ken Whisenhunt – 1962 – Professional Football Player

Robert Sean Leonard – 1969 – Actor

Tasha Smith – 1971 – Actress

Cindy Wilson – 1973 – Singer

Jason Aldean – 1977 – Country Music Singer

May 6

People Who Have Something to Say – May 6

Johann Joachim Becher – 1635 – German Chemist, Physician, and Adventurer

"The chemists are a strange class of mortals, impelled by an almost insane impulse to seek their pleasures amid smoke and vapor, soot and flame, poisons and poverty; yet among all these evils I seem to live so sweetly that may I die if I were to change places with the Persian king."

Alain Rene Lesage – 1668 – French Satirical Dramatist

"I am happy and content because I think I am."

Grove Karl Gilbert – 1843 – Geologist

"Knowledge of nature is an account at bank, where each dividend is added to the principal and the interest is ever compounded; and hence it is that human progress, founded on natural knowledge, advances with ever increasing speed."

Sigmund Freud – 1856 – Neurologist and Psychiatrist

"Civilization began the first time an angry person cast a word instead of a rock."

Harry Golden – 1902 – Writer and Newspaper Publisher

"The only thing that overcomes hard luck is hard work."

Theodore H. White – 1915 – Political Journalist, Historian, and Novelist

"Whether a man is burdened by power or enjoys power; whether he is trapped by responsibility or made free by it; whether he is moved by other people and outer forces or moves them – this is the essence of leadership."

Orson Welles – 1915 – Director, Writer, and Actor

"Create your own visual style . . . let it be unique for yourself and yet identifiable for others."

John Barrie – 1917 – British Actor

"You got kids cheating their way to a diploma and a degree. They're building a fairly shaky academic foundation."

Willie Mays – 1931 – Professional Baseball Player

"In order to excel, you must be completely dedicated to your chosen sport. You must be prepared to work hard and be willing to accept constructive criticism. Without one-hundred percent dedication, you won't be able to do this."

Bob Seger – 1945 – Rock and Roll Singer, Songwriter, and Musician

"I never say never, because I don't want to be one of those guys."

Tony Blair – 1953 – Youngest Prime Minister of the 20th Century

"I can only go one way. I've not got a reverse gear."

Roma Downey – 1960 – Irish Actress and Producer

"What you need to know about the past is that no matter what has happened, it has all worked together to bring you to this very moment. And this is the moment you can choose to make everything new. Right now."

George Clooney – 1961 – Actor

"The only failure is not to try."

Others Who Share Your Day – May 6

Pope Marcellus II – 1501 – (Marcello Spannochi)

Pope Innocent X – 1574 (Giovanni Pamphilj)

Chapin Aaron Harris – 1806 – Dentist

Max Eyth – 1836 – German Inventor and Engineer

Robert E. Peary – 1856 – Explorer

Gaston Leroux – 1868 – French Detective, Journalist, and Novelist

Nicholas II – 1868 – Ruler of Russia

William Bowie – 1872 – Geodesist

Rudolph Valentino – 1895 – Actor

Dan Gerber – 1898 – Businessman and Baby Food Magnate

Raymond Bailey – 1904 – Actor

Kenneth Wartinbee Spence – 1907 – Psychologist

Jack Allen – 1908 – Physicist

Robert Henry Dicke – 1916 – Physicist

Patricia Kennedy Lawford – 1924 – Socialite

Paul C. Lauterbur – 1929 – Scientist

Rubin Carter – 1937 – Professional Boxer

Jimmie Dale Gilmore – 1945 – Singer, Songwriter, Actor, and Producer

Ben Masters – 1947 – Actor

Mary MacGregor – 1948 – Singer

Martin Brodeur – 1972 – Professional Ice Hockey Goaltender

Adrianne Palicki – 1983 – Actress

June 7

People Who Have Something to Say – June 7

Paul Gauguin – 1848 – French Painter and Wood Engraver

"I shut my eyes in order to see."

Robert S. Mulliken – 1896 – Chemist

"I would like to emphasize strongly my belief that the era of computing chemists, when hundreds if not thousands of chemists will go to the computing machine instead of the laboratory for increasingly many facets of chemical information, is already at hand. There is only one obstacle, namely that someone must pay for the computing time."

Jessica Tandy – 1909 – Actress

"You are richer by doing things."

Gwendolyn Brooks – 1917 – Writer and Poet

“A writer should get as much education as possible, but just going to school is not enough; if it were, all owners of doctorates would be inspired writers.”

Nikki Giovanni – 1943 – Poet

“I really don't think life is about the I – could – have – beens. Life is only about the I – tried – to – do. I don't mind the failure but I can't imagine that I'd forgive myself if I didn't try.”

Liam Neeson – 1952 – Irish Actor

“It's interesting, the more successful you become the more people want to give you stuff for nothing.”

Louise Erdrich – 1954 – Writer and Poet

“Love won't be tampered with, love won't go away. Push it to one side and it creeps to the other.”

Allen Iverson – 1975 – Professional Basketball Player

"This is the thing you dream about when you're a kid, even before getting into the league."

Anna Kournikova – 1981 – Russian Tennis Player and Model

"I think it's really important for me not to forget where I came from."

Others Who Share Your Day – June 7

Pope Gregory XIII – 1502 (Ugo Buoncompagne)

John Rennie – 1761 – Scottish Civil Engineer and Designer of Bridges, Canals, and Docks

Beau Brummell – 1778 – Socialite and Arbiter of Fashion

Sir James Young Simpson – 1811 – Father of Modern Anesthetics

Alois Hitler – 1837 – American Customs Officer and Father of Adolf Hitler

Bernhard Bang – 1848 – Veterinarian

Charles Glover Barkla – 1877 – Physicist

Karl Spencer Lashley – 1890 – Psychologist

Hope Summers – 1896 – Actress

Otto Heinrick Schindewolf – 1896 – German Paleontologist

Frederick Emmons Terman – 1900 – Electrical Engineer

Marion Martin – 1909 – Actress and Singer (Marion Suplee)

Virginia Apgar – 1909 – Anesthesiologist

Dean Martin – 1917 – Actor and Singer (Dino Paul Crosetti)

Bernard Lown – 1921 – Physician and Inventor

Charles Strouse – 1928 – Composer and Lyricist

Bernard F. Burke – 1928 – Astronomer

Virginia McKenna – 1931 – British Actress, Author, and Wildlife Campaigner

Tom Jones – 1940 – Singer (Thomas Jones Woodward)

Ken Osmond – 1943 – Actor

Clarence White – 1944 – Guitarist

Jenny Jones – 1946 – Talk-show Host (Janina Stranski)

Tomlinson Holman – 1946 – Engineer

Mark Schultz – 1955 – Writer and Illustrator

Juan Luis Guerra – 1957 – Dominican Singer

Prince – 1958 – Singer and Composer (Prince Rogers Nelson)

Mike Modano – 1970 – Professional Ice Hockey Player

Karl Urban – 1972 – Actor

Bear Grylls – 1974 – TV Personality (Edward Michael Grylls)

Adrienne Frantz – 1978 – Actress

Bill Hader – 1978 – Actor, Writer, and Producer

Larisa Oleynik – 1981 – Actress

Michael Cera – 1988 – Actor

Allison Schmitt – 1990 – Swimmer

June 15

People Who Have Something to Say – June 15

Rachel Jackson – 1767 – Wife of 7th US President Andrew Jackson

"Believe me, this country (Florida) has been greatly overrated. One acre of our fine Tennessee land is worth a thousand here."

Erik Erikson – 1902 – Psychologist

"What was Freud's Galapagos, what species fluttered what kinds of wings before his searching eyes? It has often been pointed out derisively: his creative laboratory was the neurologists office, the dominant species hysterical ladies."

Saul Steinberg – 1914 – Cartoonist and Artist

"I am among the few who continue to draw after childhood is ended, continuing and perfecting childhood drawing – without the traditional interruption of academic training."

Herbert Simon – 1916 – Mathematical Social Scientist

"Everyone designs who devises courses of action aimed at changing existing situations into preferred ones."

Morris K. Udall – 1922 – Congressman

"Lord, give us the wisdom to utter words that are gentle and tender, for tomorrow we may have to eat them."

Mario Cuomo – 1932 – Governor of New York

"You campaign in poetry. You govern in prose."

Waylon Jennings – 1937 – Country Music Singer and Musician

"Don't ever try and be like anybody else and don't be afraid to take risks."

Helen Hunt – 1963 – Actress

"I think that all of us are 5-year olds and we don't want to be embarrassed in the schoolyard."

Ice Cube – 1969 – Songwriter, Actor, and Director (O'Shea Jackson)

"I think the worst thing you can do about a situation is nothing."

Others Who Share your Day – June 15

William Butler Ogden – 1805 – First Mayor of Chicago

Harry Langdon 1884 – Comedian and Actor

Georg Wust – 1890 – German Oceanographer

Hubertus Strughold – 1898 – Father of Space Medicine

Max Rudolph – 1902 – Conductor

James Robertson Justice – 1907 – British Actor

Tom Adair – 1913 – Writer for TV

Bob Wian – 1914 – Founder of Restaurant Chain

Thomas H. Weller – 1915 – Scientist

Marshall Field IV – 1916 – Businessman

Olga Erteszek – 1916 – Lingerie Company Owner

John Bennett Fenn – 1917 - Chemist

Erroll Garner – 1921 – Jazz Pianist

Belinda Lee – 1935 – British Actress

Demis Roussos – 1946 – Greek-Egyptian Singer

Jim Varney – 1949 – Actor

Craig C. Culver – 1950 – Restaurateur

Karen Morrell – 1954 – Educator and Author

James Belushi – 1954 – Actor

Polly Draper – 1955 – Actress, Writer, Producer, and Director

Julie Haggerty – 1955 – Actress and Model

Eric Heiden – 1958 – Olympic Speed Skater

Eileen Davidson – 1959 – Actress

Courtney Cox – 1964 – Actress

Tory Burch – 1966 – Fashion Designer

Leah Remini – 1970 – Actress

Jake Busey – 1971 – Actor and Producer

Neil Patrick Harris – 1973 - Actor

Billy Martin – 1981 – Author and Guitarist

Nadine Coyle – 1985 – Irish Singer

August 19

People Who Have Something to Say – Aug 19

John Dryden – 1631 – Poet and Dramatist

"Words are but pictures of our thoughts."

Samuel Richardson – 1689 – British Novelist

"Calamity is the test of integrity."

Bernard M. Baruch – 1870 – Economist and Advisor to the US President

"Most of the successful people I've known are the ones who do more listening than talking."

Orville Wright – 1871 – Printer, Publisher, Airplane Inventor

"No flying machine will ever fly from New York to Paris."

Coco Chanel – 1883 – Fashion Designer

"Fashion changes. Style remains."

Leonid Kulik – 1883 – Mineralogist

"The results of even a cursory examination exceeded all the tales of eyewitnesses and my wildest expectations."

Ogden Nash – 1902 – Author and Poet

"A family is a unit composed not only of children but of men, women, an occasional animal, and the common cold."

Malcolm Forbes – 1919 – Publisher

"Being right half the time beats being half-right all the time."

Gene Roddenberry – 1921 – Screenwriter, Producer, Aviator

"These are the voyages of the starship Enterprise. Its five year mission . . . to boldly go where no man has gone before."

Willie Shoemaker – 1931 – Professional Jockey

"Desire is the most important factor in the success of any athlete."

Story Musgrave – 1935 – Astronaut

"I had no books as a child. I had real machines, and I went out to work in the fields. I was driving farm machinery at five, and fixing it at age seven or eight. It's no accident that I worked on Hubble 50 to 60 years later."

William Clinton – 1946 – 42nd President of the United States

"We must teach our children to resolve their conflicts with words not weapons."

Matthew Perry – 1969 – Actor

"After I got my first laugh on stage, I was hooked."

Others Who Share Your Day – Aug 19

John Flamsteed – 1646 – British Astronomer

Seth Thomas – 1785 – Clock Manufacturer

Edward John Dent – 1790 – British Clockmaker

James Nasmyth – 1808 – Scottish Engineer

Lothar Meyer – 1830 – German Chemist and Discoverer of Periodic Law

Charles Hires – 1851 – Businessman

Colleen Moore – 1899 – Actress

James Gould Cozzens – 1903 – Novelist

Eddie Durham – 1906 – Jazz Musician

Philo Farnsworth – 1906 – Inventor and TV Pioneer

Joseph Hoffman – 1909 – Biophysicist

Willard S. Boyle – 1924 – Physicist

Debra Paget – 1933 – Actress (Debralee Griffin)

Alan Baker – 1939 – British Mathematician

Jill St. John – 1940 – Actress

Johnny Nash – 1940 – Singer and Songwriter

Fred Thompson – 1942 – Politician, Attorney, and Actor

Eddie Raven – 1944 – Country Music Artist

Charles Wang – 1944 – Businessman

Charles F. Bolden, Jr. – 1946 – Astronaut

Tipper Gore – 1948 – Wife of US Vice President Al Gore (Mary Elizabeth Aitcheson)

John Deacon – 1951 – British Musician

Peter Gallagher – 1955 – Actor, Musician, Writer

Adam Arkin – 1956 – Actor

John Stamos – 1963 – Actor

Kyra Sedgwick – 1965 – Actress

Lee Ann Womack – 1966 – Singer and Songwriter

Tabitha Soren – 1967 – Journalist

Clay Walker – 1969 – Country Music Artist

Erika Christensen – 1982 – Actress

Tammin Sursok – 1983 – Actress

October 10

People Who Have Something to Say – Oct 10

Hugh Miller – 1802 – Scottish Geologist

"Nature is a vast tablet, inscribed with signs, each of which has its own significance, and becomes poetry in the mind when read."

Lyn Yutang – 1895 – Chinese Writer and Editor

"No one realizes how beautiful it is to travel until he comes home and rests his head on his old, familiar pillow."

Helen Hayes – 1900 – Actress

"The hardest years of life are those between ten and seventy."

Clare Boothe Luce – 1903 – Congresswoman and Ambassador

"Courage is the ladder on which all the other virtues mount."

James Clavell – 1924 – Author

"The search for the truth is the most important work in the whole world, and the most dangerous."

Nora Roberts – 1950 – Author

"You don't find time to write. You make time. It's my job."

Wendy Wasserstein – 1950 – Playwright

"Don't live down to expectations. Go out there and do something remarkable."

Tanya Tucker – 1958 – Singer

"When I was younger, I thought about retiring."

Brett Favre – 1969 – NFL Football Quarterback

"Life deals you a lot of lessons, some people learn from it, some people don't."

Others Who Share Your Day – Oct 10

Henry Cavendish – 1731 – British Chemist

Benjamin Wright – 1770 – The Father of American Civil Engineering

Thomas Drummond – 1797 – Scottish Civil Engineer

Giuseppi Verdi – 1813 – Italian Opera Composer

Sir John Simon – 1816 – British Pathologist

Paul Kruger – 1825 – State President of South African Republic

Earle Dickson – 1892 – Inventor of Band-aids

Lester Germer – 1896 – Physicist

Lilly Dache – 1898 – French Milliner and Fashion Designer

Jane Winton – 1905 – Actress and Opera Soprano

Ivory Joe Hunter – 1914 – Rhythm and Blues Singer, Songwriter, and Pianist

Thelonious Monk – 1917 – Jazz Pianist and Composer

Ed Wood – 1924 – Screenwriter, Producer, Director, Author

Richard Jaeckel – 1926 – Actor

Gerhard Ertl – 1936 – Chemist

Chris Tarrant – 1946 – British Radio and TV Broadcaster

Ben Vereen – 1946 – Actor, Singer, and Dancer (Benjamin Augustus Middleton)

Jessica Harper – 1949 – Actress, Singer, and Author

Julia Sweeney – 1959 – Actress

Jodi Benson – 1961 – Actress

Mario Lopez – 1973 – Actor

Jodi Lyn O'Keefe – 1978 – Actress and Model

Dale Earnhardt, Jr. – 1974 – Race Car Driver

Mya – 1979 – Singer, Dancer, and Actress (Mya Marie Harrison)

October 20

People Who Have Something to Say – Oct 20

Sir Christopher Wren – 1632 – British Astronomer and Geometer

“A time will come when men will stretch out their eyes. They should see planets like our Earth.”

John Dewey – 1859 – Philosopher, Psychologist, and Educator

“Education is not a preparation for life; education is life itself.”

Bela Lugosi – 1882 – Actor

“Every actor is somewhat mad, or else he'd be a plumber, or a bookkeeper or a salesman.”

Evelyn Waugh – 1903 – British Writer

“We cherish our friends not for their ability to amuse us, but for ours to amuse them.”

Arlene Francis – 1907 – Actress

"Trouble is a sieve through which we sift our acquaintances. Those too big to pass through are our friends."

Art Buchwald – 1925 – Newspaper Columnist

"Whether it's the best of times or the worst of times, it's the only time we've got."

Joyce Brothers – 1927 – Psychologist and Newspaper Columnist

"Listening, not imitation, maybe the sincerest form of flattery."

Mickey Mantle – 1931 – Professional Baseball Player

"Somebody once asked me if I ever went up to the plate trying to hit a home run. I said, 'Sure, every time.'"

William Christopher – 1932 – Actor

"I've often wondered about people that come to the profession late in life. I've wanted to be an actor since first grade. I watched a play being performed by the third grade class, and it was . . . magic."

Christiane Nusslein-Volhard – 1942 – German Geneticist

"I immediately loved working with flies. They fascinated me, and followed me around in my dreams."

Lewis Grizzard – 1946 – Comedian and Columnist

"The game of life is a lot like football. You have to tackle your problems, block your fears, and score your points when you get the opportunity."

Tom Petty – 1950 – Singer, Guitarist, and Songwriter

"Most things I worry about never happen anyway."

Viggo Mortensen – 1958 – Actor, Musician, Poet, and Photographer

"Any ordeal that you can survive as a human being is an improvement in your character, and usually an improvement in your life."

Snoop Dogg – 1971 – Actor (Calvin Broadus)

"If it's flipping hamburgers at McDonald's, be the best hamburger flipper in the world. Whatever it is you do you have to master your craft."

Others Who Share Your Day - Oct 20

Vannoccio Biringuccio – 1480 – Italian Metallurgist and Practitioner of Pyrotechnical Arts

Austin Flint – 1812 – Physician and Pioneer of Heart Research

George Robert Stephenson – 1819 – British Railroad Engineer

Arthur Rimbaud – 1854 – French Poet

Charles Ives – 1874 – Composer of Classical Music

Sir James Chadwick – 1891 – British Physicist

Charley Chase – 1893 – Comedian, Actor, Screenwriter, and Director

Ellery Queen – 1905 – Author of Detective Fiction (Frederic Dannay)

Bob Sheppard – 1910 – Announcer for Professional Sports Teams

Barney Phillips – 1913 – Actor

Fayard Nicholas – 1914 – Tap Dancer

H. Tracy Hall – 1919 – Chemist

Herschel Bernardi – 1923 – Actor

Brown Meggs – 1930 – Screenplay and TV Writer

Eddie Harris – 1934 – Jazz Musician

Bill Chase – 1934 – Trumpet Player

Jerry Orbach – 1935 – Actor

Jeff Smith – 1939 – Chef

Hilda Solis – 1957 – US Secretary of Labor

Lynn Flewelling – 1958 – Author

Les Stroud – 1961 – TV Personality

Jonathan I. Schwartz – 1965 – Businessman

Dan Fogler – 1976 – Actor and Filmmaker

John Krasinski – 1979 – Actor

Alona Tal – 1983 – Actress

November 17

People Who Have Something to Say – Nov 17

Hans Zinsser – 1878 – Bacteriologist

"Lice, ticks, mosquitoes and bedbugs will always lurk in the shadows when neglect, poverty, famine or war lets down the defenses."

Eugene Wignor – 1902 – Physicist

"It is nice to know that the computer understands the problem. But I would like to understand it too."

Soichiro Honda – 1906 – Businessman and Founder of Honda

"Success is 99 percent failure."

Rock Hudson – 1925 – Actor (Roy Harold Scherer, Jr.)

"I'm notorious for giving a bad interview. I'm an actor and I can't help but feel I'm boring when I'm on as myself."

Martin Scorsese – 1942 – Director

"There is no such thing as simple. Simple is hard."

Danny DiVito – 1944 – Actor

"I'm always studying and I've been doing it for a long time now."

Tom Seaver – 1944 – Professional Baseball Pitcher

"There are only two places in the league – first place and no place."

Howard Dean – 1948 – Politician and Physician

"We have to say what we believe . . . whether it's popular or not."

Daisy Fuentes – 1966 – TV Personality and Model

"To do a really good interview, you have to be truly interested in the person."

Rachel McAdams – 1978 – Actress

"I have a certain curiosity for life that drives me and propels me forward."

Others Who Share Your Day – Nov 17

Nicolas Lemery – 1645 – French Pharmacist

Nicholas Appert – 1749 – French Confectioner and Inventor of Airtight Food Preservation

Louis XVII of France – 1755 – King of France

Sir John Evans – 1823 – A Founder of Prehistoric Archeology

William Anthony – 1835 – Physicist

George Beilby – 1850 – Scottish Chemist

William Burton – 1865 – Chemist

John Plaskett – 1865 – Canadian Astronomer

Grace Abbott – 1878 – Social Worker and Activist

Lee Strasberg – 1901 – Actor and Director

Les Clark – 1907 – Walt Disney Productions Animator

Geoffrey Bourne – 1909 – Anatomist

Harry Ackerman – 1912 – TV Executive

Shelby Foote – 1916 – Novelist

Stanley Cohen – 1922 – Scientist

Alan Curtis – 1934 – Harpsichordist and Conductor

Gordon Lightfoot – 1938 – Musician

Auberon Waugh – 1939 – British Columnist

Lauren Hutton – 1943 – Model and Actress

Lorne Michaels – 1944 – Producer (Lorne Michael Lipowitz)

Solomon D. Trujillo – 1951 – Businessman

Yolanda King – 1955 – Motivational Speaker and Writer

Susan E. Rice – 1964 – United Nations Ambassador

Leslie Bibb – 1974 – Actress and Model

Laura Wilkinson – 1977 – Diver

Isaac Hanson – 1980 – Singer and Instrumentalist

Kat DeLuna – 1987 – Singer and Dancer

Shanica Knowles – 1990 – Singer and Actress

BIOGRAPHIES

Gustavo Terceros is a kid who goes to Spring Creek Academy. He is also known for writing Facts of Alaska, Alien Sightings, and the marsupials Koalas. Gustavo is fairly good with a computer and can do many things with one. Although he is only 12 years old, he is already an uncle of 2 (and soon to be of 3). Gustavo was also born in the middle of the year and the middle of the month, also known as June 15.

Gustavo has many people who help him with his work at home and school. He is even extremely allergic to many things in the world, so Gustavo doesn't get to go outside much but still finds a way to have fun. He is learning to play the piano in his free time while he is at home. Gustavo always like to go to the movies with his father when he's around. He goes with his brother to many places in the car. He hopes you enjoy reading the information of koalas, Alaska and alien sightings he has gathered for you!

Brad Dalke lives in the beautiful city of McKinney, Texas. He plays a lot of sports but his best is golf. He has already given a verbal commitment to the University of Oklahoma for golf. In the summer of 2010, he won the U.S. Kids World Championship in Pinehurst, North Carolina by four shots. His scores were 68, 68, 68.

His parents went to the University of Oklahoma as well. His father played linebacker on the 1975 National Championship football team. His mother was on the women's golf team. He currently goes to Spring Creek Academy in Plano, Texas. After school, he goes to the Jim McLean Golf Center in Fort Worth, Texas. His role model is Phil Mickelson because Phil is a very successful golfer and is very loyal to his fans. He would stop at any time to sign autographs. Brad wants to be just like him.

Brad and his other 7th grade classmates at the Spring Creek Academy are writing this book. Brad wrote the Overwhelming Oklahoma, Weird Things Sold on eBay, Most Expensive, Super Bowl, and Weird Town Names.

Henry Thomas, the author of the "Weird Phobias", "Emoticons", and co author of "Dumb quotes", is the first of his family to be born in Texas, and has lived in Texas for all of his around 4000 days of his life. Henry has always been a thinker of what's out there, a philosopher of what is, and always thinking of things he will never know for sure the answer to. He plays competitive chess (yes, there is such thing) as his most accomplished hobby. Once he played in an international chess tournament in Nashville, Tennessee.

He plays guitar as a hobby. Henry also admires nature and all the natural wonders that surround him. He loves architecture, especially by Frank Lloyd Wright's architectural style. Wight did many very famous buildings including, Falling Water, The Guggenheim Museum and many more organic architectural works. His fundamental mindset was to build around nature, not through it. In the end, Henry is proud to be a part of this book, and to have the privilege to explore, to learn, and to discuss his findings with the other seven participants. He hopes you enjoy the book. :-)

Maya Gonzalez is thirteen years old and lives in the Dallas/Fort Worth area with her parents and her very fluffy pets. She is a competitive dancer and dances everyday except for Sunday. Her dance studio goes to many competitions and conventions every year.

Maya loves dance conventions because she gets to take classes from other people and get a new style from all the different teachers, for example at the last convention she went to she got to meet tWitch, from So You Think You Can Dance. She's an actor and a singer. What she wants to do in life is to be a star on Broadway.

When ever she has spare time Maya likes to read a good book while listening to her playlist "Calming" on her iPod. She currently attends Spring Creek Academy in Plano, Texas, but hopes one day to move to New York, where she hopes to attend Julliard or Columbia. She is a vegetarian and has been one her whole life. She is also a gymnast at ASI gymnastics.

Maya loves going to other places and other states and cities all around the U.S. where you get to do new things. One of her favorite things is to take a trip, for being on an airplane or a car gives her more time to read. For her last birthday she asked for gift cards to bookstores. She loves rain, and also dancing, singing, walking, sitting, or just being in the rain. Why? Because it is like music.

Nikki Leondis is 13 years old. She was born in Scottsdale, Arizona. She now lives in Frisco, Texas and goes to school at Spring Creek Academy. Nikki is an actress who has been in several movies including the major motion picture "Igor". Her other hobbies include dancing three times a week, playing tennis, singing, and is starting modeling. She has many achievements and can't choose her favorite.

When she gets older she plans to go to New York University. She loves New York and goes there all time. When she is there she loves shopping on 5th Avenue and watching plays on Broadway when she's there.

One of Nikki's role models is her uncle who is a movie director. He is a role model to her because he had the guts to fly out to L.A. to pursue something he loved and she inspires to be like him. Although she isn't sure what she wants to be when she gets older, it's ok, because right now she is only worried about the present.

Nikki loves her many friends who she hangs out with all the time. She lives with her mother, father, brother, and her new puppy. Her heritage is Greek and Italian, and she can speak Spanish, and some Greek. She loves traveling all over the world. One of her favorite spots is the Cayman Islands.

Nikki is also very adventurous. She has been on wave runners countless amounts of times, loves water skiing, and so much more. But her favorite of all time is shark diving. One day she plans to bungee jump. Writing this book has been very fun for her and she hopes to do another one in the near future.

Joshua Evers lives in the Dallas area of Texas. He is 11 years old and attends 7th grade at Spring Creek Academy in Plano, Texas. His favorite subject is history. He lives with his parents and an older brother. Some of his hobbies are cooking, competing in taekwondo, playing the piano, and also playing and competing in chess. For fun, he enjoys playing with friends and technology, and spending time with his pet snake.

One of his favorite things in the world is reading. And as much as he likes reading, he likes writing books. Knowledge to Joshua is not just priceless, but a requirement. If there was anything he could learn more about, Joshua would want to know more about science. Another thing very important to Joshua is music. Listening to music and playing music to him is extremely important.

When Joshua grows up, he hopes to write more books. His lifelong goal is to publish a book that becomes a famed classic tale. Some of his favorite kinds of literature are mythology and fiction. As long as Joshua can, he hopes to write more books and even a few series.

Another of Joshua's favorite things is to go on vacations. His favorite vacation spot is Hawaii. He hopes one day to go to Europe. Another one of Joshua's favorite things is serving in his school's student council. He enjoys every moment of helping his school and student council.

Joshua contributed the Dumb Crooks, Dumb Warnings, Weird Laws, and Texas Facts sections of this book. Joshua and his class wrote this book for a school project. Joshua found the experience of writing a book enjoyable, entertaining, and most of all, fun. On a scale of 1 to 10 in enjoyment, Joshua would say a 10. Writing small stories and books are extremely enjoyable to Joshua, and he hopes to write many, many more.

Nick Fichter is currently living in Dallas, Texas, and is attending Spring Creek Academy. Nick is the author of Arizona. He is a guitarist who enjoys most music. Nick has played guitar for about 7 years now. He enjoyed playing at the House of Blues and other locations around Dallas including his mom's bar and restaurant, "LaGrange".

Nick's role models for music include Slash, Chris Cornell, and Nuno Bettencourt. In Nicks' guitar lessons, he enjoys learning songs, learning about the music theory, and writing songs and guitar solos.

Nick also enjoys playing many sports. His favorite sport is hockey; even though he hasn't played it in a long time, Nick is looking to start it again. He was also very good at basketball. Once Nick played on a fifth grade team that would have won the playoffs, but they were beat by a team of eighth graders.

Nick has a sister who is always doing something crazy, a baby brother, and a baby sister. Nick enjoys school and hopes we get to write more books like this in Language Arts.

He also enjoys spending time with his family and going down to Austin to see his dad where every weekend Nick is down there, something crazy happens. Someday he wants to live in Hawaii, San Diego, or the cruise ship that sails around the world 24/7.

Last, Nick says that someday he wants to do good things for the world with his music and he wants to revolutionize the music industry.

REFERENCES

Most of the research for the development of this book was conducted using Internet sources. The primary references used are:

www.hubpages.com

www.ehow.com

www.biography.com

www.infoplease.com

www.thinkexist.com

www.findingdulcinea.com

www.dumblaws.com

www.legendsofamerica.com

www.buzzle.com

www.travelchannel.com

www.dumbcriminals.com

www.britannica.com

www.brainyquotes.com

www.blogspot.com

www.todayinsci.com

www.famouswhy.com

www.legendsofamerica.com

www.pashnittours.com

www.awesomeamerica.com

www.theamericanpeopleencyclopedia.com

www.californiatravelexpert.com

www.corporate.disney.go.com

www.great-disney-vacation.com

www.diszine.com

www.hiddenmickeys.org

www.goflorida.about.com

www.wdisney.com

www.disneycruisenews.com

www.bukisa.com

www.funnynames.com

www.dumblaws.com

www.dumbwarnings.com

www.dumbcrooks.com

www.enchantedlearning.com

www.ingramcontent.com/pod-product-compliance
Ingram Content Group UK Ltd.
Pitfield, Milton Keynes, MK11 3LW, UK
UKHW041942190726
13854UKWH00004B/1736

9 780578 077857